WHAT ABOUT WINNING IN LIFE NOW

"I believe the philosophy Michelle Prince shares in Winning in Life Now can make a significant difference in your life."
Zig Ziglar, Author & Motivational Speaker

"Michelle Prince has taken the foundational truths of life and shared an action-oriented plan that closes the gap between mediocrity and success. A must read for the individual who is serious about building a successful, well-rounded life."
Bob Alexander, Speaker, Trainer, Author & President - The Alexander Resource Group

"Michelle Prince has put together a power packed book full of proven, real world strategies that will change your life. Stop waiting, start winning, read this book."
Mike Litman, #1 Best-Selling Author
Conversations with Millionaires

"Michelle's book is going to change lives worldwide! Winning in Life NOW is an exceptional book that will engage you with every word as you learn how to live a successful happy life. Get ready for a breakthrough to LIVE a happier life right now."
John Di Lemme, International Motivational Speaker

"Are you ready to throw away your excuses and make the most of your life? Then Michelle's book is for you! By applying the principles in this book, you will find more happiness, develop the confidence to become all you were born to be, and live a life filled with purpose. You will start Winning in Life Now!"
Tina Downey, Founder of MySuccessBox®

"Michelle has brought a dose of reality to words that people can relate to and be inspired by. She is living proof that we are limitless and success can happen as long as you believe."
Troy Rackley, Success Coach

"How many of us are walking down roads that are leading nowhere?" asks Michelle Prince in her dynamic book, Winning in Life NOW. Here is a positive upbeat approach to showing us how we can stop making excuses for leading only a half-life. Step by Step, Michelle guides us through the process of taking corrective measures for creating the life we've always wanted."
Carol Adler, President/CEO Dandelion Books

"We all know that tomorrow will be better, that we'll change tomorrow, or that we'll 'fix it' tomorrow. That works great – if only tomorrow was guaranteed – but it's not. That's why Michelle Prince's Winning in Life Now is a must read…..NOW! In Winning in Life Now, Michelle shares her life experiences with a down to earth, easy to understand perspective of the importance of NOW. A fresh voice in the motivational and inspirational arena has arrived."
Rick Hagler, Author of *It'll Be OK & Motivational Coach*

"I've had the privilege of knowing Michelle since we were 18 years old and freshmen in college. I can attest that Michelle has personally used her philosophy throughout the years and has been an inspiration for me to use that philosophy in my own life. Being there to experience her personal growth is a huge testament to the outcome of her book and the goals she's made AND accomplished throughout the years."
Kami Schiller, Account Executive Dell Computers

"Michelle Prince uses her unique experiences and down to earth style to give us a refreshing look at how to achieve true success in life. This book isn't about a 'quick fix' to happiness; it is about working hard and doing the right things to get what you have always wanted. Thanks, Michelle, for sharing the experiences on your own journey and for giving us a plan of action to achieve our own dreams."
Jill Hellwig, Key Account Executive, Ziglar, Inc.

"The author of this book is a testimony to the truth you will find inside these pages. She is someone I have watched apply these principles to her life and has continually risen to the top. You can rest assured if you take these words to heart….you too, can start winning now."
Melissa Hovendick,
Vice President of Sales Amber Pharmacy

"As a busy mother of three children, I do not have much free time. Michelle's book was easy to read, and it truly inspired me to make some positive changes in my life. When I feel overwhelmed I remember her words and it gets me back on track to keeping my life where I want it to be NOW."

Christine Cocca, Mother & President of Woman's Club

"The content of this book clarifies, reminds and inspires you to keep thinking, believing and working to create goals…to create the life dreams are made of. I have met the author and had the great blessing of hearing her thoughts about this book…about her desire to make a real difference in other's lives. That has made it easy as well as a pleasure to be able to encourage others to read this book. She is a wife, mother, daughter, professional and a seeker of truth. With all the demands these place upon her, her vision was to inspire and help her fellow human beings. She is living proof of what she puts forth in this book for all, for you to read. Maybe you have read many, many books, listened to records, tapes and now CDs for years. Perhaps you are new to this search for guidance. Whatever place you find yourself; this book is one you must have. You will not find one written with more sincerity of purpose."

James Heath, Rehabilitation Specialist

Winning In Life Now

How to Break Through to a Happier You!

Steph,
You are a winner!
Michelle

Michelle Prince

Copyright © 2009 Michelle Prince

Performance Publishing
McKinney, TX

All Worldwide Rights Reserved, McKinney, Texas

All rights reserved. No part of this publication may be reproduced, stored in a retrieval system or transmitted, in any form, or by any means, electronic, mechanical, recorded, photocopied, or otherwise, without the prior permission of the copyright owner, except by a reviewer who may quote brief passages in a review.

ISBN: 978-0-615-26354-0

www.winninginlifenow.com

Contents

Foreword By Zig Ziglar 13
Introduction 15

Chapter One: Living On Purpose 19
    Are You Stuck In a Rut?
    Are You Afraid of Change? 21
    Define Your Goals 22
    Do Our Dreams Ever Really Go Away? 22
    You-You-You 23
    What Is Your Passion? 24
    Questions To Ask Yourself 25
    New Year's Eve Goal Setting 26
    Keep It Simple! 27
    Live Like You're On a Mission 28

Chapter Two: Believe It Or Not! 31
    Victors Or Victims? 32
    The Power of Belief 33
    Unexpected Surprises 34
    Born To Win—At What? 36
    Believe It To See It! 38
    You Are In Control 39

Chapter Three: What Were You Thinking?..................41
    The Power of Positive Thinking 42
    Feel How It Feels; See How It Looks................43
    Unfounded Romance Anxieties........................46

Chapter Four: How Much Are You Worth? 51
    Scarred Illusions...53
    The Self-Esteem Barometer.............................53
    The Big Self-Esteem Question 54
    The First Stop On the Road
    To Building Self-Esteem Is Self-Love................55
    Working Things Out 56
    Mirror, Mirror On the Wall 57
    How To Overcome People Pleasing 58
    Who Are You, Really? 60
    Save the Mask For Halloween! 61
    "The Real Me" NatalIe Grant 63
    Love Yourself!..64
    Selfishness Vs. Self-Responsibility 65

Chapter Five: Balancing Act 67
    Too Much Is Too Much. 68
    Life Is A Series of Choices. 70
    Your Daily Goals...75
    Is Your Wagon Empty Or Full? 77
    Knowing Is Half the Battle...............................78

Chapter Six: Don't Worry-Be Happy 81
   We Get To Choose How We Feel. 83
   Half Empty Or Half Full? 83
   What's On Your Unhappiness Laundry List? 84
   Place Those Negative Feelings Into the Washing Machine and Add Plenty of Detergent 85
   Decide To Be Happy and
   Witness The Change. 86
   The "Happy If" Syndrome 87
   Gratitude—The Twin Sister/Brother
   of Happiness 88
   Focusing On Good Things
   Makes Us Feel Good 89
   The Gift of Receiving 91
   Laughter—The Greatest Gift of All 92
   Is There A Secret To Happiness? 95

Chapter Seven: Get Started Now! 97
   Who's Calling the Shots? 98
   Practice Discipline and Motivation 99
   Dust Off Your Dreams 100
   What Are You Waiting For? 103
   Start Living Now! 104
   Live Each Day To the Fullest 106
   Why Wait? 107
   The Last Lecture 108

Chapter Eight: Keep On Keeping On! 111
    Get Out of Bed! 113
    It Starts With You 115

About The Author 117
Michelle's Favorite Motivational Products 119

DEDICATION

TO my husband, Chris, and our two boys, Austin and Tyler, who continue to be the inspiration in my life. Thank you for your support and love.

To my parents, John and Ellen Arnott, who taught me to follow my dreams and never give up. Thank you for your wisdom, love and encouragement.

Foreword by Zig Ziglar

WE were privileged to have Michelle Prince on the staff at Ziglar for about three years. During that time Michelle brought her delightful personality and high energy level to our sales efforts. She developed her skills and solid character traits into a strong, mature, idealistic and enthusiastic woman who has learned to put feet to her own potential. *Winning in Life Now* is a testament to her passion to lead and enable others to become more than they have ever hoped or believed possible.

Michelle has done a superb job of condensing some of the most life-changing information on goal setting and life balance available into basic steps that are easy to understand and apply. She clearly sets out the "whys," explaining the critical element of balance for success in every life area. She presents solid foundational principles upon which to build, while offering psychologically sound advice.

Winning in Life Now can make a significant difference in your life, *if* you are sincere in your desire to grow, develop and change, and willing to take the steps necessary to do so.

Introduction

THROUGHOUT my life, I have read inspirational books, listened to motivational CDs and attended many personal development seminars. If not for the encouragement, as well as the treasure trove of power-tips and techniques these materials provided, I would probably still be asking myself what a purposeful life would look like, and how I can have one.

I'm far from being an expert in any of the areas I write about; rather, I come from the perspective of a student who has done the work, taken the notes and attended the classes. It is through this journey that I've discovered ways to improve my life, and it is my hope that my experiences will help you to do the same.

I've been asked why I titled the book *Winning in Life Now*, rather than just *Winning in Life*. After all, isn't that what we all want? To be winners throughout this journey of life? I decided to add the word "Now" to stress the urgency with which we must live each day, each moment, in order to be truly happy.

The word "now" is as old—and young—as we are. Earliest languages used only present tense. The past was gone, so it wasn't possible to live there, and the future had not yet happened; therefore, it was still non-existent.

Only later did we add two more tenses to our language, giving us two more lifestyle choices. We could live in the now, creating our reality day by day and moment by moment; live in the past by holding onto it and pretending it still existed; or live for a time that has not yet happened, pretending that "things will be better."

Although many of our inspired teachers continue to remind us that *there is only the now*, that doesn't mean that everyone is ready and willing to accept this notion. Denial can be so much more comfortable! A nagging or nostalgic past and fairytale future often keep us enthralled for the major part of our lives.

"Winning in life" joins the reality of *now* with a game plan that acknowledges lessons from the past. It also encourages us to create our own future—step by step, moment by moment.

Have you ever considered the fact that you cannot win unless you lose? Or: let's talk about the polarities of light and dark or hot and cold. Would we ever know what light looks like unless we've experienced darkness; or what cold feels like unless we feel as if we're burning up inside, and dripping with perspiration?

Life is all about contrasts. In this book we will remove the competition factor from "winning" and demonstrate the value of embracing both winning *and* losing as the foundation for acknowledging self-love, self-esteem, and self-worth.

Once we learn how to love and appreciate ourselves, we can appreciate all that life has to offer. At that point, we're ready to choose how we want to feel, think, behave and act. We turn the key in the ignition and rev up the motor.

Are you ready to start creating a winning life *now*?

Chapter One

Living on Purpose

In the late eighties, one of my favorite movies was *Made in Heaven*. The film starred Timothy Hutton and Kelly McGillis as two people who fell in love while in heaven, but were separated when Annie (Kelly McGillis), who had not yet earned her wings on Earth, had to leave on a tour of duty and put in time inhabiting a human body.

Mike (Timothy Hutton) is beside himself with despair, but the heavenly powers offer him a deal. Mike can return to Earth, but only on the stipulation that he and Annie will not remember each other. They are given thirty years to find one another.

Back on earth in a physical body, Mike can't seem to get his act together.

There must be something more to life, an inner voice keeps insisting. *There must be a reason why I'm here.*

The harder Mike tries to ignore that inner voice, the more persistent it becomes. Then one day he meets some people who sense that Mike is struggling to unleash a strong inner desire. It seems to be connected to Mike's love of music and to fragments of a song that keep playing over and over inside his head.

In order to better express this song, Mike teaches himself how to play the saxophone. To his delight, the more skillful he becomes as a saxophone player, the more fragments of the song he brings forth. Ultimately, it is Mike's magnificent saxophone performance of the song in its entirety that reunites him with Annie.

To this very day, I can still remember the words of Mike's song. It was as if at that point in my life, they struck a chord in me because I needed to hear them. From that time forth they have served as a powerful reminder:

> *"If you don't really know where you want to go, it makes no difference which road you take."*

How many of us are walking down roads that are leading nowhere? How many of us have a feeling that our lives could be happier and more prosperous but *our current circumstances are holding us back and making it impossible for us to succeed?*

The *Made in Heaven* "Mike" didn't know where he was going, because he didn't know what he wanted. Because he didn't have a purpose, he didn't really care where he ended up.

Could that Mike (or Mary) be you?

I think many of us are so busy moving through our lives, that we don't stop long enough to ask whether there is a purpose behind all of this activity. We wake up, go to work, pay the bills, and simply exist—doing the same thing day in and day out because *we think it's what we should be doing.*

Often we don't bother dreaming about what we want in life because we're stuck in the rut of thinking we need *this job, this relationship, this life.* It's comfortable, and change is—well, scary.

Are you stuck in a rut? Are you afraid of change?

If you fit the "stuck in a rut" description, I want to reassure you that there *is* something better for you and for every person who feels they are missing out on something. You really can have so much *more*:

- Happiness
- Peace
- Joy
- Success
- Self-satisfaction

It all starts by knowing what you want and then living *on purpose.* *Purpose* is the goal or intended outcome of something. It's a destination or a process that leads to achieving what you want in life.

Define your goals

A lot of people don't have purpose, direction or even motivation to move toward what they want, because they haven't defined what "that" is. They don't have goals. How many times have you heard someone say, "I don't know," when asked, "What do you want to do in life?" or, "Where do you see yourself five years from now?"

Ask that same question to preschoolers and they'll rattle off a whole list of things they want to be or do when they grow up. They know exactly what they want. No one has shattered their dreams or stomped on their hopes.

"Wise adults" will shake their heads and smile knowingly. "Wait until you grow up and meet the real world," they're thinking. It's sad but true that many adults give up on their dreams because they let them get crushed by the realities of bills, mortgages, raising a family, and all the other pressures of being an adult.

Do Our Dreams Ever Really Go Away?

If you reach into your deepest memory pockets, I bet you'll still find those same dreams tucked away, just waiting for you to pull them out and dust them off.

Who said you couldn't have your dreams come true or live a life that is hopeful, happy, and secure? I'm guessing it wasn't anyone in particular—or maybe it was a family member or other adult you looked up to during your growing years—someone who you thought "knew better."

Their dreams hadn't come true; they hadn't ever achieved any of *their* goals. Didn't that mean, therefore, that *no one else in their circle of close friends and family could ever experience these "miracles" either?*

Has anyone ever held a press conference on your life and announced that you can't accomplish your dreams and that "you can't make it happen," "you're not good enough"… "don't even bother trying"? I don't think so!

The fact is, the only person who may have lost faith in your goals is *you*. But the good news is the only person who can change your life around is *you*!

You-you-you

It all starts with deciding:

- what *you* want
- where *you* want to go
- what *you* want to have, and
- how *you* want to live.

In other words, *it starts with deciding to live on purpose.*

Okay, okay. I can hear your whispers, mutters, mumbles, and groans: "Easier said than done, Michelle."

Isn't that what you're thinking?

You: "I want to make my goals happen but I don't have the time, the money, or the skills to do what needs to be done. Plus, it sounds like a lot of hard work."

Me: That depends on what you mean by "hard work."

Remember Mike in *Made in Heaven*? He loved music; *he had a passion for it.* He really wanted to learn how to play the saxophone. Do you think those long hours of practice were tedious for Mike? Do you think he considered them "work"?

Ask anyone who loves what they do whether they consider it work, or joy.

You have everything within you right now to be the best *you* that God created. You were perfectly created just the way you were supposed to be, in order to fulfill a purpose here on earth.

Finding and then living that purpose, as Mike discovered, is not only possible for each of us; it is our mission. It is why we are here on earth in a physical body.

What is your passion?

What do you want to *be, do*, and *have*?

My mentor, Zig Ziglar, says, "You've got to *be* before you can *do*, and *do* before you can *have*." In other words, having what you want is not as easy as snapping your fingers. First you have to do the work (e.g., learn how to play the saxophone or go through the necessary training to become a nurse/dancer/lawyer/fireman/professor, etc.).

We transform the "being" into "becoming" by turning our work into accomplishments.

Questions to ask yourself

- What are you doing today to be that person you want to be?
- Are the actions you're taking today leading you toward or away from your goals?
- How much time do you spend reading about successful people versus watching television?

The fact that you are reading this book tells me that you want more for your life and you are willing to do what it takes to make it happen.

World renowned motivational authors and speakers, including Zig Ziglar, Jim Rohn, Brian Tracy, Denis Waitley and more, have created wonderful goal-oriented seminars and programs that are also available as books, CDs, DVDs, and downloadable products on the Internet. These programs take you step-by-step through the goal-setting process, and then mentor you toward your destination.

Shop around and choose a program that fits your lifestyle and budget. It really doesn't matter which one you choose; what *does* matter is that you choose one, and then start moving forward!

New Year's Eve Goal Setting

Every New Year's Eve we have a family tradition of writing down our goals for the next year. I have two small boys who are now in elementary school, but when I began this practice, they were in preschool.

Each of us receives a sheet of paper with the assignment of writing down five things we personally want to *be, do* or *have* in the coming year: what we want to accomplish, where we want to go—anything we can think of that defines what we want to make happen.

We also set three goals that cover the same *be, do* or *have* concept for us as a family. Each of us goes to a different place in the house to spend time thinking about what we will write down. Then after dinner, while we're waiting to watch the New Year's ball drop on Times Square in New York City, we read our papers aloud.

It's always fun and interesting to see what my little ones come up with. Some of the goals are silly to us adults, but to the children they are extremely important, and can be anything from getting to play on the soccer team to getting an award at school or going to Walt Disney World.

One year my oldest son wrote that he wanted to get his Green Belt in Karate. At the time, he was fairly new to Karate and the Green Belt was several belts away from his current position. I'm proud to say he met that goal with many months to spare. He knew what he wanted and went after it. To really want something is powerful.

It's possible that he could have received his Green Belt without writing down his goals, but maybe not. Maybe he would have given up after receiving his first belt if he didn't have anything else to reach for. The truth is, we will never know. What we do know is that he set a goal and he got what he wanted. Mission accomplished.

The best part of this tradition is seeing the belief and confidence on my kids' faces (as well as us adults) when they can check off that goal and know they have the power to make their dreams a reality.

Keep it simple!

- Take an afternoon away from work or the kids, and spend some time alone really thinking about your life.
- Look at where your life is today and where you want it to be.
- Write down dreams for yourself with no worry about whether they will come true or not. Just get them on paper.

My friend Tina Downey, creator of the MySuccessBox® system, recommends writing one hundred dreams for your life. Here's how to do this:

1. Think only about what you want, and not about how you will get there.
2. Narrow those dreams down to your *number one current dream.*
3. Focus only on the steps you can take that will move you in the direction of achieving it.

Colossians 3:2, in the Bible, says, "Set your mind on things above." If you set your mind on what you desire in life, you will move toward those desires.

If you focus on what you don't want in life, that's exactly what you will get. It's all about deciding what you want and then living a life of purpose to make it happen.

Have you ever heard someone describe a person who is walking really fast, "as if they're on a mission"? That's you!

Live like you're on a mission.

Live like you know where you're going. Live the life you know you were born to live. Get started today by:

- Writing down what you want in life
- Deciding when you want to achieve each of these desires

- Believing you will achieve everything on your list

Amazing things happen when you believe.

Chapter Two

Believe It or Not!

Keep your dreams alive. Understand to achieve anything requires faith and belief in yourself, vision, hard work, determination, and dedication. Remember all things are possible for those who believe.
—Gail Devers (Olympic Gold Medalist)

MOST of you have heard of *Ripley's Believe It or Not* books and museums; or maybe you've seen the TV show. Ripley's is a collection of crazy and sometimes grotesque images of people doing outrageous things.

Many of the images are really "unbelievable," which explains the greatness of the title. We know they are true, but it's hard to believe that someone would or could actually do those things.

Have you ever had that *Believe It or Not* feeling yourself, when something happens in your life that seems unbelievable? Maybe it's a divorce or death in the family; or maybe it's losing your job, your house, or something else you didn't see coming. However, the fact that you didn't believe it was possible didn't change the fact that it happened. *Believe it or not, it just was.*

We cannot control the lives of others, just as we cannot control events such as earthquakes and other natural disasters. We can, however, choose to believe these events are part of a master plan and that there is a greater power at work on our behalf. Or, we can believe the opposite: that the world is out to get us.

Victors or Victims?

We can be positive, trusting beings, or victims.

I personally choose to believe that everything, good and bad, happens for a reason and that my grand plan is unfolding each day of my life, "believe it or not."

If you've ever driven across the country, you know what it's like to be sailing along at the maximum speed limit for long stretches, with little traffic on a well-paved, four-lane highway. Then, suddenly without warning, the detours occur: road construction, a bridge out, a traffic accident ….

This is a picture of daily life. Often a detour will lead us away from where we thought we were going—onto a totally new road. Or it will delay our trip because of unforeseen circumstances.

You can either enjoy the ride, potholes and all, or get angry and upset—maybe even feel frustrated enough to turn around and go back.

The power of belief

Fear keeps us from our dreams; faith moves us toward them.

I was eighteen years old, about to attend my first year of college at the University of North Texas. A typical teenager, I had many friends, and my main joy in life at the time was hanging out with all of them and having fun.

Because it was my last weekend before I left for college and most of my friends were leaving home to attend schools in other parts of the state, both days were crammed with parties and get-togethers. I was certainly looking forward to this weekend of fun! I had picked out my outfits for each party, and every detail was arranged down to the last minute.

My mother knocked on my bedroom door. "Honey, we have a special gift for you and John (my brother)." Smiling sweetly, she announced, "We've just purchased tickets for an amazing motivational seminar that we're so eager for both of you to attend."

I whirled around and stared at her, unbelieving. *A motivational seminar! Kill me now!*

I was furious, and that is an understatement. I couldn't believe I was being forced to go to a seminar that I had no interest or desire to attend. The worst part—far worse than having to sit through the seminar—was having to miss out on the last big weekend blast with my friends.

I knew better than to argue with my parents, because

I learned at a very young age that they were in charge, and no amount of whining would do anything to change their minds.

John also had plans for the weekend, so he wasn't thrilled either.

We arrived at the seminar early, so before going inside, I remember we sat in the car and discussed the idea of ditching it altogether. Nope. That didn't seem like a good idea after all, because we knew our parents would find out somehow, and it wasn't really worth the consequences.

We'd both learned from past experiences about "consequences." My parents were loving disciplinarians, and now as a parent myself, I'm grateful they were, and also very understanding!

Unexpected Surprises

To this day, participating in the seminar instead of turning around and heading back home for a weekend of partying, was one of the best decisions I've ever made.

The seminar, "Born to Win," was hosted by Zig Ziglar. It occurred over the course of three full days, and the topics included goal setting, self-esteem, positive mental attitude building, and many other valuable tools that are basic to constructing a purposeful life.

The seminar room was packed with adults. John (at the age of twenty) and I (only eighteen) stuck out like sore thumbs. These people were looking for "more" in their lives, and at this point in our development, my brother and I hadn't even started to "live" in order to know what "more" might look like! So far, our parents had protected us from the real world of bill paying, families to feed, mortgages, job losses, career changes, relationships, etcetera.

Surrounding the stage where Zig and his team would facilitate the conference were several tables. John and I picked seats in the back of the room hoping to sneak out if we could. People at our table were very friendly and certainly not condescending, so we were made to feel comfortable.

Shortly after the seminar began, Zig asked everyone to look under their chairs for a number that would identify the table where we would be seated for the rest of the conference.

Whoosh! Away went my security blanket of having my big brother next to me; away went my chance to bolt for the closest exit. And what a good thing *that* turned out to be!

At my assigned table of strangers was a group of people who were thrilled and grateful to be attending this seminar. The weekend tuition and hotel fee was a hefty one, and I soon learned that for many it was a financial stretch. That didn't seem to matter. These eager participants were more than willing to do what it took in order to have an opportunity to participate in a Zig Ziglar event.

Their enthusiasm was contagious and I soon found myself also getting excited. Although for a teenager the seminar sessions seemed over-long and intense, their content was life-changing.

At the conclusion of the weekend, I realized with great amazement, joy, and gratitude, that I was a changed person. That was almost twenty years ago. The teachings of Mr. Ziglar and his staff established the foundation for my future life as an adult.

I now understand why so many adults applauded me and praised my parents for gifting us with this valuable experience at the outset of our lives. These people, then in their forties and fifties, were obtaining information for the first time, that John and I, just starting out, had an opportunity to use for the rest of our lives.

The weekend was so inspiring to me; I made a commitment at that moment to follow in Mr. Ziglar's footsteps: to change people's lives the way this amazing man had changed mine.

At the end of the seminar, I walked up to Mr. Ziglar, shook his hand, looked him straight in the eye and vowed, "I'm going to work for you someday!" I believed this with all my heart.

I was eighteen at the time, and I made it happen at age twenty-three.

Born to win—at what?

I had a very successful run in college; I graduated with high honors, was president of my sorority, and in those four years, collected an impressive list of achievements. In retrospect, I know this would not have been possible had I not attended the "Born to Win" seminar.

And then life began. At the time I graduated, the job market was poor. I had some skills in sales, but I didn't want to be a "salesperson" for the rest of my life. So—what else could I do?

My confidence in myself dropped when I couldn't find a job. I was used to achieving what I set out to do, and eventually I caved and took a job selling Minolta office copiers. My base salary was only $12,000 a year, with the expectation that I could make ten times that in commission. In reality, I didn't make a penny over my base.

The job involved a lot of door-to-door cold calling on businesses. Every week we would swap territories with a co-worker in order to have an opportunity to help one another. One particular week I swapped territories with the rep who had Carrollton, Texas.

As I pushed through the doors of one of the businesses my co-worker suggested I visit, I realized it was The Zig Ziglar Corporation. I couldn't believe my eyes!! Although I had attended a Zig Ziglar seminar in Dallas, I had no idea that his corporate office was in nearby Carrollton, Texas. I was so flustered when I approached the receptionist's desk, I think I managed to say something like, "Is this really where Zig Ziglar works? Do you have any job openings? I'll do anything!"

BELIEVE IT TO SEE IT!

What greater proof of the power of positive, purposeful intention! I'd stated to Zig Ziglar himself that I wanted to work with him—that was my goal—and here I was, blurting out my intent to his receptionist!

She said they were just finalizing some interviews that week but no offers had been made yet, so I still had a chance to submit a resume. I asked what the position was, and to my disappointment, it was for a salesperson. When I weighed the desire to leave a career in sales versus having a chance to work for Zig Ziglar, the latter won out.

That night I prepared a resume, which was sparse, as I could only list my current job of six months and some sales jobs in college. I faxed the document to the receptionist and prayed that I'd hear from her. To my delight, the next morning I had a call from the Vice President of Sales, asking to schedule an interview.

After the interview I was offered the job, and of course, I accepted. *I had told Zig Ziglar I would work for him someday, and now it was coming true!*

Some might say this was a coincidence; I happened to be in the right place at the right time. Yet I know, at a deeper level, that something else was going on. It all started with belief—and desire. I knew what I wanted; I expressed that desire *and believed it was going to happen.*

Belief can open doors for you that you might not have even known were there.

- Know what you want and why you want it.
- Believe you will then get what you want.

I have to tell you that the silver spoon didn't just slip into my mouth. No way! I had just begun my test drive and I would encounter many speed bumps along the way. These challenges tested both my goal setting and Positive Mental Attitude (PMA) skills that I'd learned at the seminar, but I also learned about stamina and perseverance. I didn't let anything interfere with my dream.

You Are In Control

Life can take a lot from you, but it can't take away your dreams. *You have complete control over your thoughts, attitudes, and actions.*

You are the only person who can make you feel depressed or rejected. Only you can tell yourself that you're worthless. You might hear these statements from other people, but *you* are not *those people*. Whatever *they* think, say, or do is their opinion, their statement, their action.

Only you can tell yourself what you want to feel.

- If you want to feel powerful, tell yourself you have power.

- If you want to feel successful, start acting the way successful people act.

You will have challenges; everyone does. In fact, we create those challenges ourselves in order to meet and surmount them. As mentioned in Proverbs, without grist for the mill, the wheel will not turn!

- Believe in yourself and you will be able to keep that wheel turning.
- Believe in your dreams and you will find yourself always moving forward.

I want to share with you one of my favorite poems about belief. During my college years, it helped me to believe that I could accomplish whatever I set out to do. Even now as an adult, I still embrace the message this poem delivers.

…Believe in yourself and in your plan;
Say not – I cannot – but, I can.
The prizes of life we fail to win
Because we doubt the power within
—Author Unknown

Chapter Three

What Were You Thinking?

THOUGHTS have power. They drive our decisions, our goals, our dreams, and ultimately our lives. Are you living the life you've always dreamed of living? If not, then *what were you thinking?*

What were you telling yourself all these years to get where you are today? Did you believe you were worthy of success, or did you have some doubts about your future?

What did you tell yourself you could or could not do? What did you tell yourself you wanted to accomplish? *When did you decide that what you wanted wasn't within your reach?*

It happened the moment you first thought it couldn't happen.

Thoughts are more powerful than most people think, because they are private. We don't see the harm in beating ourselves up when we make a mistake, or telling ourselves we aren't good enough. We may not even realize that we're always talking to ourselves.

Every instant we're alive, we are unconsciously sending signals to our brain to tell it how to function. Many of the obstacles we face are in our minds.

We dwell on every possible reason for how we could fail, and spend little or no time focusing on how we could win!

When I was in college, I gained the "Freshman Fifteen." For those of you who are unfamiliar with the term "Freshman Fifteen," it means I gained fifteen pounds during my first year in college.

Late night pizza, little exercise, and … well you know how it goes. Soon those jeans don't seem to fit right. And then it's the t-shirts and dresses. This was devastating to me, because I'd always been slim and never had to be concerned about my weight.

Added to the Freshman Fifteen was the Sophomore Ten and then—you guessed it: the Junior Ten. *Yikes!* I felt like "Large Marge," as my friends and I used to say.

The Power of Positive Thinking

Finally I had the motivation to do something about it, with the help of Dr. Norman Vincent Peale's famous book, *The Power of Positive Thinking.* Dr. Peale talks about the power of thoughts.

"Imagine yourself in the state that you desire," he writes. In my case, I had to imagine myself at the weight where I felt and looked my best. I also had to imagine myself doing the work to get there. I had to see, tell, and train myself to envision the exercise I would do to get my weight down.

I was home for the summer, so every evening I dedicated myself to walking/running around the block. This gave me a good workout, because the block around my parents' house was approximately one mile. I'd warm up walking, and then gradually begin running.

At first, I could only run for a minute or so. I used to count houses to see how many I could pass while I ran. I can remember only making it past two houses in the beginning. Two houses! Then I started to see myself getting to the third house, then the fourth, then half way around the block, until finally, all the way back to my starting point. It took some time to get myself back in shape, but little by little I did get there.

Feel how it feels; see how it looks

I also thought about how I would feel if I were thinner and in shape. Those thoughts really drove my motivation.

My mind went with those thoughts and found a way to make it happen.

The mind is like a child; it wants to please. It wants to do what you tell it to do. I told myself I was thin and that I could run around the block without stopping. I felt how it felt; I saw how it looked. I even envisioned what I was wearing as I ran lightly and effortlessly in my new body size. It became a reality because I believed it was already *my reality.*

I became what I thought about and believed.

Have you ever known someone to do something really foolish? You ask, "What were they thinking?" How much easier it is to see how thoughts determine the actions of others than it is to see this in ourselves! "If they were thinking clearly, they would not have done such a thing," we say to ourselves.

So, what about us? *If we were thinking clearly …!*

Exercise #1

On a piece of paper, write down all the things that you're telling yourself. Include both the good as well as the bad—things that are so ingrained in your mind; you don't even know they're wrong.

For example:

- I'm not worthy of love.
- I don't deserve to be successful.
- I'll never have enough money.
- I could never do what he/she does.
- My life is never going to change.

We tell ourselves so many false and limiting beliefs; we actually start to believe them!

I've always struggled with my own self-worth and self-esteem. My limiting beliefs included statements such as, "I'm not good enough"; "I'm not pretty enough"; or, "No one would ever love me if they knew the real me." This type of self-talk crushed my dreams and hopes for many years, until I finally realized they were holding me back.

I also had a fear of success. In a way, I felt guilty if I was successful, and especially if I made a lot of money. I had a negative idea of what "rich" people were like: snotty, arrogant, aloof, and alone. I didn't want to have any of those traits, so subconsciously I thought; *I don't want to be rich.*

Of course, all these thoughts were so far below the surface of my subconscious, I didn't even realize I'd been thinking them for so long, and ultimately sabotaging my opportunities for success or love.

Until I was twenty-one years old, I had such a belief that I wasn't good enough; I felt I needed fixing in order to qualify, or "pass the test." Of course, I didn't really know what that test was or what my standards were, and that's what made these beliefs so foolish and irrational.

Unfounded Romance Anxieties

I *knew* I would have a *terrible time* finding someone who I thought loved me. (Notice the italicized words—the self-talk I was constantly delivering!)

I spent so many years trying to please others, doing what I thought *they* wanted *me* to do. Yet I never spent time figuring out what *I* wanted to do. I'd date, but because I wasn't being real with myself, I'm sure guys saw that, and didn't stick around long. Fortunately, my husband, whom I've been with for the last 16 years, changed that limiting belief.

I had just decided to give up on guys when I met Chris. It was my senior year in college and the idea of finding Mr. Right was long gone. We were introduced by a mutual friend at a local hangout. He was nice, but it didn't cross my mind that I might go out with him. After all, I was ready to join the convent at that point.

I discovered that he lived across the parking lot from me in my apartment complex. All these years of never seeing him on campus or at our complex, and then suddenly I saw him everywhere! He was very sweet and persistent, even though at first I was standoffish. I guess because I wasn't trying to impress him or be someone I thought he would like, he fell in love with the real me: the *me* that I thought wasn't good enough!

We started to date after a few weeks of just being friends and we dated five years before we got married. During those five years we got to know and trust each other for who we really were.

My self-esteem did not improve overnight, but as I grew more aware of my internal dialogue, I practiced replacing negative, unwanted thoughts and beliefs with positive affirmations.

Exercise #2

Now that you have your list of limiting beliefs, practice replacing each negative statement with a positive one. Write these positive statements on 3x5 index cards, one per card. Here are some examples of negative thoughts/beliefs and how to turn them into positive statements:

Negative:	**Replace with:**
"I am not worthy of true love."	"I deserve to be unconditionally loved."
"I am ugly."	"I am beautiful in the way God made me. I am his perfection, his masterpiece."
"I'll never be rich."	"I love making money; I am prosperous and deserve to be wealthy."

Exercise #3

For the next thirty days, once in the morning, and again in the evening, look at yourself in the mirror and repeat each of your new positive affirmations with enthusiasm and conviction.

I guarantee by the end of the thirty days, you will see a change in your attitude, your thoughts and your life. This exercise works because it uses the power of our all-powerful minds. What we tell ourselves is the fuel that lights our fire.

The choice is always ours: whether we want to make our fire blaze with a flame that is bright and steady, or let it burn down to a pile of smoldering ashes that eventually die out.

After you've completed the exercises, I'd love to hear from you to know how you were able to transform some of your limiting beliefs about yourself to positive affirmations.*

You have just made the first step toward taking complete charge of your life. By identifying negative thoughts and self-talk, and replacing them with positive ones, you've turned up the flame and ignited your fire-and-desire to create a happier, more productive and satisfying life. You're well on your way to winning at life—not somewhere in the far distant future—but *right now!*

*Email me at info@princeperformance.com or visit my website and blog at www.winninginlifenow.com.

Chapter Four

How Much Are You Worth?

RECENTLY I saw an interesting news report about a famous model who decided to get her legs insured. Her legs were a highly marketable asset, so it was important to her and her modeling agency to make sure they would be protected against any potential injury or harm.

Her right leg was insured for $600,000, but her left leg was "only" insured for $500,000. A hundred thousand dollars is a big difference for the same set of legs! The reason for the price difference was because her left leg had a tiny scar on it. The insurance assessors felt that because of the scar, the left leg was not as "valuable" as her other leg.

I'm not in the insurance business or the modeling world, but it struck me as odd that someone's legs could be insured. It seemed even stranger to me that one leg was worth less than the other because of a tiny scar.

If just her set of legs alone are worth $1,100,000, I

wonder how much they think the rest of her is worth. And then, the big question:

Who is really qualified to determine the worth of an individual?

Obviously, this model has a healthy self-esteem to consider her legs so valuable—or at least her agent or business manager has provided this "value" for her in terms of dollars and cents.

What about you? If someone were to take out an insurance policy on you, how much would you be worth?

Of course I'm using this illustration as a metaphor. Obviously, we cannot place a price tag on our worth. This is just a way of demonstrating that whenever we measure ourselves against someone else's standards, our "flaws" or "scars" immediately become apparent.

I'm sure many of you, like me, have "scars" that make us feel that our value is less than it should be. Maybe we've made mistakes, been deeply hurt by someone, or possibly have hurt someone ourselves.

It doesn't make any difference whether our scars are physical or emotional; anything that varies from the accepted norm that is considered a "10" or "perfect" by The Professional Flaw-finder Crew can make us feel that we're not good enough, nor worthy of success or happiness.

These "scars" may be so enormous in your eyes, they successfully hide the beauty within you—or, to put it another way, you are hiding your beauty behind those scars. When you hide behind a scar, your thoughts, beliefs, feelings, and behaviors cover up that wonderful you.

Scarred Illusions

These scars are not real and they are not "you." They are just representations of the struggles you've gone through in life. It is these struggles, however, that provide the friction we talked about earlier. They are the grist for the mill that can ultimately motivate and inspire you to improve your life and change how you see yourself.

Your past challenges represent the strength and determination you demonstrated during those trying times, and your value as a human being is even more elevated because of those "battle scars." They are marks of valor that show how far you've come, and how much stronger and wiser you are today, as a result of having met those challenges instead of running from them.

Our level of self-esteem depends on the value we give ourselves. Our self-worth depends on how we see ourselves—not through the eyes of someone else, but through our own eyes.

The Self-Esteem Barometer

If we allow our level of self-esteem to depend on circumstances, from one moment to the next it can soar upward or zoom down toward the lowest reading on our self-esteem barometer. Johnny just scored the winning goal in a soccer game, so he may have very high self-esteem after the game. However, Johnny's self-esteem may shoot downward if he can't score any goals during the next game.

The objective of the larger game of life is to have high self-esteem readings all the time, regardless of our circumstances.

Some people make a distinction between self-esteem and self-worth.

Self-esteem refers to the impression we have of ourselves based on performance and response to life's challenges.

Our intrinsic value or self-worth, on the other hand, is a core value that simply is. It does not depend on behavior or any type of character demonstration. It is who we are and who we were born to be. We have value, simply because we exist on the planet in physical form. Nothing can change or take this value away from us.

It's easy to forget or ignore the wonderful you that was created for a specific purpose on this Earth. *It's easy to overlook the fact that you're perfect just the way you are—and that whatever you label a "scar" is actually a medal of honor.*

If we are perfect creations of God, then why do we feel so bad about ourselves?

The Big Self-Esteem Question

If one of your friends or co-workers made a mistake, would you berate this person by calling her an idiot or making her feel worse? Of course you wouldn't. You know she's only human, and we all make mistakes.

You'd likely tell her not to worry about it and console her to make her feel better.

Why, then, do we beat ourselves up over making the same mistakes? Why do we focus on our flaws and weaknesses? Why do we have so little compassion or understanding for ourselves? Why do we show respect and forgiveness toward others, but not to ourselves?

Check in with your self-esteem for the answer to these questions. Self-esteem affects every area of our lives.

Our barometer reading of self-esteem has a direct correlation to our projected levels of success. Why is this so?

The first stop on the road to building self-esteem is self-love.

The ability to love, accept, forgive, and believe in ourselves plays a huge role in determining our level of self-esteem.

Our relationship with ourselves is the most important one we will ever have in our lives. It is more important than the relationship with our parents, spouse, or even our children. Our relationship with ourselves also affects all other relationships, so if you don't love yourself, you will not be able to love anyone else.

This statement bears repeating: ***If you don't love yourself, you will not be able to love anyone else***.

Working things out

Self-love and self-esteem are closely bonded to each other. When you don't believe in your abilities, your value or your worth, your mind cannot respond in the opposite way. Your mind will go in the direction of your dominant thoughts. If you don't feel good enough, you will likely live a life to confirm these beliefs.

If I asked you to list ten positive qualities about yourself, could you list all ten immediately? Or, would you get stuck after the third or fourth one? What if, on the other hand, I asked you to list ten of your worst qualities, or things you don't like about yourself; do you think you could complete that list much faster? The fact is, *most of us focus on what's "wrong with us" rather than what's "right about us."*

Twelve-year-old girls going through puberty usually struggle with some form of low self-esteem. It's a time of physical, as well as emotional change. The fear and uncertainty of "what this new life is all about" can trigger feelings of self-doubt that could send the self-esteem barometer soaring downward. What if another issue were also causing low self-esteem?

Mirror, mirror on the wall

A girl I knew in junior high was beautiful, but she had a tiny bump on her nose. This bump was barely noticeable to anyone else, but it was very noticeable to her. She would look in the mirror and only see her nose. She would avoid acknowledging her big blue eyes, long blonde hair, and bright smile. All she saw was that bump, and it made her feel like the ugliest girl in school.

In conversation, she didn't speak with a lot of confidence. She didn't feel she was as pretty as the other girls, so her actions followed suit. She did not spend much time with friends, because she never thought they really liked or accepted her. Throughout her junior high years, she kept to herself.

As this girl grew and started high school, other people, especially boys, started to notice her. She was strikingly beautiful, and over time she came out of her shell. She made lots of friends and was very popular. By the time she graduated, she was voted Most Beautiful and she was also the Prom Queen.

What do you think happened to this girl's bump? Did she get plastic surgery to remove it? No! Not at all! The bump is still in the same place and just as noticeable or unnoticeable as ever.

What changed was how this girl saw herself.

She began to see what everyone else was seeing. She

was gorgeous because of who she was, and not because of her nose or her outer appearance.

No matter how pretty someone can be, if the inside doesn't match, no one will notice the outside. In this girl's case, everyone noticed her inner *and* outer beauty. Many of the kids in school would have been shocked to learn that this girl had low self-esteem because she was popular, outgoing, and appeared to be happy. On the inside, however, she saw herself differently.

What caused the change? I'm guessing that an "act as if" factor played an important part in making the shift from "poor me" to "amazing and wonderful me." When this girl "appeared" to be happy, she played the role of being happy until indeed she was! That inner joy transcended a nose bump and sent her onto the dance floor with the rest of her classmates.

"Fake it until you make it" is a favorite expression among those who know and understand the power of our thoughts, feelings, and actions.

How to overcome people pleasing

Others who are outgoing and appear to be happy may not practice faking it until they make it. Inside they remain miserable and broken. Often they need others to validate their worth.

People who try to be the center of attention can sometimes have the lowest self-esteem. Because they need to feel accepted by others, they're willing to forego their own self-acceptance. This is a heavy price to pay. Ultimately we learn that if we live to please others, there's no way to be true to who we really are.

People with high self-esteem generally don't feel the need to impress others or gain their approval. They feel okay just the way they are.

Those who struggle with low self-esteem and low self-worth also have the "not good enough" syndrome. They fear they won't be accepted by others because they don't qualify, so they spend most of their energy figuring out what other people want them to be. Then they try to become that type of person.

If they think they can only be accepted when they're friendly or happy, then they do everything possible to make sure everyone knows how happy they are. You'll never find these people complaining or admitting how they really feel. It's always "Great!" "Wonderful!" "Couldn't be better!"

I'm embarrassed to admit but I was that "happy person" in my teens. I wanted to fit in; I wanted everyone to like me. I figured if I was nice and sweet that no one could find anything about me that they didn't like. I was always smiling and was friends with just about everyone. Outwardly it seemed to work, but inwardly it was a totally different story.

Who are you, really?

I can recall my senior year in high school, receiving many awards and honors, but the two that struck me most were "Most Friendly" and "Most Courteous." Most people would have felt great being thought of as the friendliest person in the entire senior class, but I felt very differently.

The day I received those honors I went home with tears in my eyes because I didn't feel like I was the friendliest or most courteous person. I felt like I just convinced everyone that I was, which meant no one knew the *real me*.

Like most teenagers, I sometimes felt angry and resentful toward people, but was too scared to show it. I'd never speak my mind for fear that I'd disagree with someone, and that would cause them to not like me.

Sadly, I just told others what they wanted to hear. This made lots of people like *me* but it made me not like *myself* very much.

There was a girl in our class that was mean, and bullied many of the other girls. I'm not sure how I ended up in her circle of friends, but she considered me one of her best. I can remember her telling me that she didn't like a particular girl because she disagreed with her opinion.

She made a comment about how this girl used to be so nice and everyone liked her until she finally got tired of being agreeable and started to speak her mind.

This girl told me that if I ever changed the way I

acted, stopped being happy, supportive and friendly, that everyone would hate me, too. It was at that moment I was certain that pretending to be happy was better than losing friends.

Fortunately, this thought pattern was short-lived. I quickly realized how wrong this was so I changed that belief. I no longer lived to be popular but rather to be real.

Thankfully, I've been blessed with the most loyal, supportive, and loving friends throughout my entire life. These true friends have always accepted and liked me on my good *and* bad days. It's through these friendships that I got over the need to be liked by *everyone,* and became grateful just for my *real* friends.

But, what about those who never had any *real* friends? Many people, maybe even you, still believe they aren't good enough, so they pretend to be someone they are not.

Save the mask for Halloween!

Wearing a mask is very strenuous; there's always the chance of being found out, and eventually that's what happens. When we're not on our best behavior or guarding our emotions, the transparency leaks through.

You may know someone who seems to be good-natured all the time. He's the kind of person you like to be around because he always has a positive attitude. Then one day you learn that he's taken his life, or in a rage, he's injured or killed others.

When you don't know who you really are, you don't know what you really want. All you know is what others want from you.

Consider the logic: How can you really be accepted if you don't know who you are? How can anyone really like you if they don't know the real you?

One of my favorite songs is called "The Real Me," by Natalie Grant. The words are very powerful to me because I've always been a "people pleaser" myself. Here are the lyrics:

"The Real Me"
Natalie Grant

Foolish heart looks like we're here again
Same old game of plastic smile
Don't let anybody in
Hiding my heartache, will this glass house break
How much will they take before I'm empty
Do I let it show, does anybody know?
[Chorus:]
But you see the real me
Hiding in my skin, broken from within
Unveil me completely
I'm loosening my grasp
There's no need to mask my frailty
Oh, Cause you see the real me
Painted on, life is behind a mask
Self-inflicted circus clown
I'm tired of the song and dance
Living a charade, always on parade
What a mess I've made of my existence
But you love me even now
And still I see somehow
Wonderful, beautiful is what you see
When you look at me
You're turning the tattered fabric of my life into
A perfect tapestry
I just wanna be me

The words by themselves don't do the song justice because they are set to a beautiful melody. I never tire of listening to it.

Can you relate to this song? Can you relate to the fear of being yourself? The fear of revealing the core of who you were made to be? Have you played this game for so long that emotionally you're breaking inside and don't know how much longer you can go on hiding behind masks?

If so, break free! Release yourself and love yourself for who you are, just as you were made to be. Let go of the fear of being judged.

Love yourself!

You've probably heard the well-known command from the Scriptures: "Love your neighbor as yourself." Its intent is to teach people how to treat others. Actually, this is another version of the Golden Rule: "Do unto others as you would have them do unto you."

Treat yourself well, or just as you would treat other people (and as you would want them to treat you). Ironically, many people interpret this wisdom by beginning with their neighbor and excluding themselves in the phrase, "Love your neighbor." Period. What happened to "love yourself"?

We focus on the needs and desires of others. We give and we give, until finally we have nothing left but neglect for ourselves and our own needs. We jump through hoops to make other people happy—but at our own expense. The end result is the feeling of being overwhelmed, exhausted, and drained of any reserve energy to focus on our own wants and needs.

Selfishness vs. Self-Responsibility

When traveling on an airplane with young children, if necessary to use the drop-down oxygen masks, adults are instructed to place air masks first on themselves, and then on their children. The logic behind this is to ensure that in the event of an emergency, the adult has enough oxygen to help the child. If the adult places the mask on the child first, there is a risk that the adult will run out of air and not be able to help themselves or the child. This would leave the child unable to fend for himself.

Is it selfish for the adult to place the mask on themselves first? No! It's just being responsible.

Take care of your own needs and desires first in order to be able to take care of others. Love yourself first and then you have the physical, mental, and emotional capacity to love others.

Give yourself quiet time, exercise, challenging work, meetings with friends—anything that recharges you as a person. By acknowledging your needs, you acknowledge your self-worth. As with the parent and the oxygen mask on the plane, what do you have to give others, if you have neglected yourself?

Loving yourself means:

- Thinking as highly of yourself as you think of friends or peers
- Celebrating your own strengths and achievements
- Forgiving yourself for your mistakes
- Focusing on what you *can* change, and not on what you *cannot* (You can't change the past, but you *can* change the way you think about your past.)
- Comparing yourself to you, and not to others ("How am *I* doing?")
- Setting up realistic expectations
- Accepting and learning from your mistakes
- Being open and assertive with what you need from others
- Accepting compliments from others gracefully

Pat yourself on the back. Be proud of who God created you to be. You are worthy because you were born. You are unique, special, and powerful.

Continue to help others. Continue to love those around you, but do so once you've loved yourself. If you are not physically, mentally, and emotionally full, you won't have anything to give to anyone else. Love *yourself* so that you can love your neighbor!

Chapter Five

Balancing Act

It is often said that balance is the key to happiness and the good life. When related to self-esteem, most of us are aware that we fill our lives with activities and obligations for others without thinking about ourselves and what we may need. There is a way to take care of yourself while also helping others.

A lot of people, mostly good friends, have asked me through the years, "How do you do it? How do you manage a full time, very time- consuming job that includes travel, while raising two kids? How do you fit everything else in as well—exercise, kids' sporting events, church activities, family get-togethers, birthday parties (not to mention your relationship with your husband)?"

Usually I joke back, "NOT VERY WELL!"

The truth is, I got really good at juggling. I figured out how to have balance in my crazy life and not drop the "balls in the air."

To be honest, I didn't even realize I had a lot on my plate until friends, who didn't work or didn't have kids, pointed it out to me. It was all I knew, so that was normal for me.

When I see a mom with triplets, I find myself asking how on earth she survives, taking care of three kids the same age! I'm exasperated just thinking about it. The typical response from the mom is usually, "I don't know any better, so I just adjust." In other words, they don't know what it's like to have one child versus having three to raise at the same time. They manage just fine with three, because it's the only way they know.

That's how I see myself sometimes. I've never really known it any other way so it's seems normal to me to work at balancing my life. I've always liked to be busy. In fact, I think I'm at my best when I have many things to juggle. I much prefer juggling to being lazy.

However, because of my ability to multi-task and keep my balance while managing a heavy schedule, I can also spread myself too thin at times. Over the years, I've recognized this and have worked very hard to maintain balance.

Too much is too much.

Doing too much of anything—eating, working, volunteering, exercising, church activities, relaxing even, becomes unhealthy. Each activity recharges or fuels the others. We can compare it to recharging our bodies with meals that are balanced, and that contain all the basic nutrients for giving us the energy we need, while at the same time, preventing the build-up of stress.

Marriage between two people whose lifestyles are out of balance often ends up in divorce. Often one of the partners spends too much time at the office and neglects his spouse and family. Or, one of the partners does not carry his share of the financial responsibility. Possibly one or both of the persons is dealing with personal issues such as substance abuse, or other co-dependent challenges, and refuses to get help.

I know all people are busy, but I think working mothers experience an extra amount of chaos. It's challenging to be pulled in so many directions simultaneously. It's easy to feel guilty when you have to be away from your family.

In my case, in the early days of my marriage, my career in sales was more lucrative than my husband's teaching career, so we didn't have the luxury of my staying home with the kids. It was the right decision for our family, and I realize some may have disagreed with our choice, but it worked for us. Nevertheless, this decision didn't make it easier for me to leave my kids each morning to go to work.

When my kids were very young, I can remember working for a company that was not accommodating to working mothers. I can recall several times dealing with tears while at work, because I couldn't leave the office to attend my son's Halloween Party or special occasion at his school. Those moments with my boys are more precious to me than anything, but at the time I needed that job to pay the bills. The reality was: sometimes I just couldn't be there.

My oldest son was affected by these job requirements more than my youngest; by the time he was one year old (my oldest was then four years old), I was able to work from home. This routine changed everything for us.

Now that I'm working from home, I can take them to and from school, volunteer in their classrooms, and do all the other things stay-at-home moms are able to fit into their schedules. I also have the privilege of working at a paying job, and I feel extremely blessed to be able to do both. We have all benefited by my career, so I'm thankful for the ability to "juggle" work and home. It can be busy at times, but it's all in how I choose to manage my schedule that makes the difference. It's all about *choosing* to have balance in your life.

Life is a series of choices.

Can you think of one thing you could do today that would improve your life? What about the opposite? Can you think of one thing you could do today that would make your life worse? It's all about choices!

Exercise

In the chart below, I have listed six core areas that make up important parts of your life. These categories include subcategories to help you to evaluate where you are in each area in terms of your level of satisfaction. Rate where you are with respect to the chart, on a scale from one to five. The highest number, five, is an area that is working great, with little room for improvement.

At the other end of the scale is number one for the area where you have a lot of work to do to get that part working right. Circle the number that most accurately describes your current state. The areas we're going to focus on are:

PERSONAL/PERSONAL GROWTH	1	2	3	4	5
Hobbies					
Reading/Growth					
Education					
Attitude					
Having Fun					
CAREER	1	2	3	4	5
Enjoy Work					
Capable					
Appreciated					
Coworker Relationships					
Ability to Advance					
RELATIONSHIPS	1	2	3	4	5
Friends/Family					
Ability to Love					
Accepting					
Good Listener					
Open Communication					
Sense of Togetherness					

FINANCIAL	1	2	3	4	5
Budgets					
Earnings					
Savings					
Investments					
Debt					
PHYSICAL	1	2	3	4	5
Exercise					
Health					
Weight					
Diet					
Stress					
SPIRITUAL	1	2	3	4	5
Inner Peace					
Church					
Belief					
Faith					
Prayer					
Purpose					

Now, I want you to take those numbers and plot them on the lines below. Next, connect the dots from the beginning of the road to the end. This is *The Road That Leads to Balance*. It will help you see which areas of your life have a few "pot holes" that need to be repaired. Some pot holes will be deeper than others, but this will pinpoint which areas of your life need extra focus and determination to make you more balanced. Eventually, we want to fill up all those pot holes and start driving on a smoother road through life.

The Road That Leads To Balance

Personal	Career	Relationships	Financial	Physical	Spiritual
5	5	5	5	5	5
4	4	4	4	4	4
3	3	3	3	3	3
2	2	2	2	2	2
1	1	1	1	1	1

Now that you have a good idea about the areas of your life where you need to do some work in order to bring them into a state of balance, I'd like you to write down at least one thing you could do today in each area that would help you start to remove some of the bumps in your road.

Maybe you could take an art class, make a phone call to your grandma, go to the gym, or eat at home rather than go out to dinner. Maybe you could make ten extra cold calls, or do something else at work that would lead to an improvement. Spend the afternoon with your kids, or volunteer in the community. The following is an example of my daily goals:

Personal:	Read thirty minutes
	Listen to motivational/inspirational CD
Career:	Finalize proposal
	Make ten extra marketing calls today
Relationships:	Plan date night with Chris
	Visit Grandma in nursing home
Financial:	Balance checkbook
	Eat dinner at home six nights this week
Physical:	Go to gym
	Thirty minutes of strength training
	Walk/run for thirty minutes or more
Spiritual:	Read Bible and devotional
	Pray with boys at bedtime

Now it's your turn. Write down one or two actions, in each category, that you can do today to bring you closer to achieving your goals.

Your Daily Goals

Personal: _____

_____

Career: _____

_____

Relationships: _____

_____

Financial: _____

_____

Physical: _____

_____

Spiritual: _____

_____

I suggest you do this exercise each day for the next thirty days, along with your affirmations. This will help you focus your day on your *priorities* rather than simply on your *to-do list*. I try to make a habit of doing this balancing exercise each morning before I do anything else.

I list a goal for the day in each area, so that I can stay balanced. I try to get these goals done before anything I have to do at work or at home. It takes discipline, but ultimately it will bring joy to your life.

Balance produces harmony, and harmony is peace. Peace is ultimately what brings us joy in life. It's all connected, but it starts with making the decision to balance out our lives first.

Please don't misunderstand the point of this exercise. It is not to add *more* work to your day, but to help you to *prioritize* your activities. Decide what you *really* want to make happen and focus only on those things.

How often do we do things that we don't want to—but feel we have to? How often do you accept party invitations or work projects that you're too busy to fulfill? You do them because you feel you "should" or because you don't want to disappoint someone.

How many times has someone asked you to help her with moving, or watching her kids, or running an errand for her, when you really didn't have the time to add this to your own *to-do list*? (You just couldn't say no!)

If you're like me, you've probably said "yes" too many times.

I used to have a hard time saying "no" to people because I didn't want to disappoint them. I wanted them to like me. I soon discovered that others learned through the grapevine that I was a "yes" person. I found myself so busy and overwhelmed; I had no time left to do the things that were important to me.

If you are too busy "being busy," you might be missing out on just the thing that could make your life happy. This is why it's good to write down one important action item per day in each area. If you run out of time after you've done all of the important things, then you know where and when to say "no."

Is your wagon empty or full?

One of the stories in Joanna Weaver's book, *Having a Mary Heart in a Martha World*, captures this point very well. The story begins with God asking a man to carry a wagon to the top of a mountain; the man happily agreed to perform this task. Along the way he encountered many people who also needed help carrying things to the top of the mountain. The man piled their things in his wagon, since he was going up there anyway.

Eventually the wagon became too heavy for the man to carry. The man then blamed God for giving him a burden that was too much for him to bear. How unfair for God to give him more than he could handle!

When he finally reached the top of the mountain, God confronted him. "Why is your wagon so full? When you started out, it was empty!"

The man explained that he was trying to help others by carrying their load to the top of the mountain. He thought God would be happy that he was helping so many people!

God responded: "Let others shoulder their own belongings. I know you were trying to help, but when you are weighted down with all these cares, you cannot do what

I've asked of you. My yoke is easy and my burden is light. I will never ask you to carry more than you can bear."

Lesson: We take on so much "stuff" in life; but that "stuff" may not be what we should be focusing on to make our lives fulfilling and happy. It's okay to say *no* to what makes you busy, and *yes* to what makes you happy!

It's a tough balance between doing what you think you should be doing and doing what's best for you in order to have true balance and freedom in life. It is this balance that brings ultimate happiness.

Knowing is half the battle

I first discovered how to manage balance in my life when I was working for Zig Ziglar. All employees participated in his "Born to Win" seminar, which was the same event I attended when I was eighteen, and had been sent by my parents. However, the second time around was even more impactful because now, as an adult, I was actually experiencing some of the challenges that Zig talked about.

Mr. Ziglar has a balance program called "The Wheel of Life." Similar to my "Road That Leads to Balance," this program identifies areas of your life that are out of balance; areas that need attention.

When I first did the "Wheel of Life" exercise, I realized I was out of balance in the financial and spiritual areas.

BALANCING ACT

At the time, I was very young, and recently out of college. I didn't have a lot of money, and I found myself living from paycheck to paycheck. Eventually, this financial stress had started to take its toll. I didn't even realize how out of balance I was in this area until I did the Wheel of Life exercise. It pointed out that I was not saving any money or making fiscally responsible decisions, and I needed to do some work to bring order to this part of my life.

"Spiritual" was the second area in my Wheel of Life that needed attention. Even though I knew it was important to me to have a strong faith, I found myself making excuses for not attending church every weekend. During this time, I was expending more effort and focus on my career and relationships. Just by becoming aware of what was really going on in my life, I was able to re-evaluate my priorities and make decisions that were in line with my beliefs.

Everyone has their own definition of balance; what is right for others may not be right for you. Evaluate each area of your life to determine what you would like to change or improve, and where you would like to direct more attention or focus.

Begin today by taking inventory of where you spend your time and energy. Then ask yourself how this list lines up with your core beliefs and long-term goals. You'll know immediately where to make those changes—and remember, "knowing is half the battle."

Chapter Six

Don't Worry-Be Happy

MANY years ago I can remember hearing for the first time the song, "Don't Worry, Be Happy," by Bobby McFerrin. It put a smile on my face immediately. Today I still smile each time I hear the song. Why? Of course, it has a good Reggae beat, but it's really the words to the song that I love. It's such a simple phrase but the impact is powerful.

What if we could go through life without worrying about money, jobs, kids, relationships, and just *be* happy?

Happiness is not a destination. It is a positive feeling of appreciation, gratitude, and contentment about our current situation. We achieve this feeling by focusing on and acknowledging all the good things in our lives.

Abraham Lincoln said: "Most people are about as happy as they make up their minds to be." It's really not so much what happens to us in life, but how we respond to those happenings.

A friend of mine, "Harry," was recently laid off from his job. He was doing a fantastic job, but the company had to cut costs, and it was mid-management that was affected the most.

Harry could have chosen to respond to this situation in a number of ways.

He could consider this downsizing as an opportunity to explore new options and broaden his horizons. He could value the severance package as a means to pay his bills while he looked for another job over the next two months. He could feel grateful for the money that would buy time to find his next great opportunity. He could consider himself an extremely fortunate person who was well positioned to move forward with his career.

Harry could also feel that he was being treated unfairly. He could spend the weeks following this devastating event thinking about the injustice of being fired, "just like that," as if he were nothing and nobody, taking it personally, and becoming so entrenched in bitterness that he couldn't even *think* of looking for another job. All his energy would be spent on feeling sorry for himself. Ultimately, this initiates a downward spiral of low self-esteem which could lead to a fear of interviewing well for his next job and even to a fear of finding any work at all. The entire eight weeks of severance could be spent focusing on victimization and what went wrong.

In this example, the details of the job layoff situation wouldn't change; the only variable would be the way Harry would choose to respond.

We get to choose how we feel.

Regardless of the situation or circumstances, we get to choose whether we want to feel happy and energized, or miserable and lethargic. Obviously, Harry will feel much better if he chooses to respond with positive energy and a plan for moving forward. Taking the low road by moaning and groaning about The Terrible Thing that just happened to him can only lead to anger, resentment and frustration. What a lot of wasted energy!

That doesn't mean the high road is easy. Often our first impulse when something unexpected happens is to tense up, burst into tears, throw a tantrum, or look for something or someone to blame. This is a typical knee-jerk response that is related to our basic survival instinct. Acknowledge this instinct and then take a deep breath.

Stop and reflect. Ask yourself: How do I want to feel? What do I want? (What is the desired outcome?) In this case, Harry would probably want a better job, possibly more challenging, with higher pay and better benefits. Fortunately, this is how Harry *chose* to respond and he went forth turning a negative situation into a positive one.

Half empty or half full?

How do you perceive that glass of water measured to the half-way mark?

A thirsty person might perceive it as filled to the brim.

A person with an abundant supply of water may not even notice whether it's half empty or half full. A person who is despondent about life in general (nothing ever goes right in my life) may not only see the glass as half empty, but with a crack. [Slowly the level of water is going down. Soon the glass will be empty. (!)]

What's on your unhappiness laundry list?

Go ahead; make that list. Here are some samples:

1. Not enough money.
2. Too busy.
3. Betsy is always in a bad mood.
4. Bruce never does want I want him to.
5. My sister acts so nasty toward me. There's no reason for her to be nasty!

What can *you do* to change each of these unhappiness items? I'll give you some hints.

1. I'm so grateful for the money we do have. I'm also grateful that we live in a world of opportunities where we can always look for ways to augment our income.
2. I enjoy managing my time well, so I never have to feel that I'm too busy to read stories to my

children, or create a wonderful bedtime experience for them when they can share all the events of the day with me.
3. I'm going to do something special for Betsy today. I know she's depressed about being overweight. I'm going to compliment her on her computer skills; she's a genius and I think she doesn't really know that.
4. Bruce is only two years old and he's eager to test his wings. I will be loving and firm with him, letting him know who's in charge. I'll make the rules into a game.
5. Repeat Number 3 with a variation. What would make your sister feel special, loved, wanted, and needed?

Place those negative feelings into the washing machine and add plenty of detergent.

How many people do you know who can still recall some of the terrible things that happened to them years, even decades ago? I know a woman in her mid-sixties who can still remember names that the "mean kids" called her in elementary school.

That's a long time to carry around that memory. I wonder if she remembers any of the compliments her grade school friends paid her.

For some reason, our minds tend to store "junk." We hold on to all the bad things that people have said or done to us through the years. Over and over in our heads, we replay tape loop of life's injustices: justifying our hurt, anger, or bitterness.

Why? Why hold on to all of that? Make a list of reasons.

Can you come up with at least one reason for keeping yourself in a state of feeling bad, resentful, angry or depressed?? What is the pay-off?

Release the junk. Make room for more joy!

Decide to be happy and witness the change.

I have a good friend who went through a divorce a few years ago. She had just delivered her third child when she found out that her husband was having an affair and wanted a divorce. The final blow was when her ex-husband announced that he was expecting a child with the "other" woman.

Can you imagine having to tell your kids that their dad is having another baby but not with their mom?

I celebrate my friend for turning these challenges into a growth opportunity. She not only maintained a friendship with her ex-husband and his girlfriend; she also warmly welcomed this woman and the new baby into her own life.

The choice was hers. She could feel miserable and defeated by the divorce, or happy and forgiving.

My friend weighed the alternative of hating her ex-husband and creating a negative, confrontational relationship with him. She did not want her children to experience this unnecessary, potentially damaging drama.

Instead, she decided to accept the current circumstances and be happy.

My friend didn't focus on what went wrong; instead, she put one foot ahead of the other and focused on what's right, right *now*.

The "Happy If" syndrome

Most unhappy people are constantly telling themselves, "I'll be happy if …" or "I'll be happy when …." "I'll be happy when I'm out of college," or "I'll be happy when I find my first job," or "I'll be happy when I get married, have a child, have another child, send my kids off to school, or when my kids go off to college." Then, it's: "I'll be happy when my kids get married and have grandkids, or when I can retire." Or: "Maybe when I win the lottery, things will change and I'll be happy!"

Soon these people are almost on their way out, and if they're lucky, they may finally have swallowed the Happy Pill. Their only question will be why they waited all these years to be happy.

Why waste an entire life waiting for what you can have right now?

It's easy to feel as if you can't be happy until everything lines up exactly the way you planned, but that is unrealistic. Life can be complicated, and often doesn't always work out the way we planned. So why keep playing the waiting game?

Are you going to be happy as you go through the struggles of life, or are you going to let the struggles take the life from you?

Make the decision to be happy now while you are in the midst of all of life's challenges. This decision won't change the circumstances, but it surely will change the way you feel.

Gratitude—the twin sister/ brother of happiness

Being thankful for what you have and who you are is critical to the way you feel about yourself and your situation. It's so easy to focus on what's going wrong, but why not be thankful for what's going right? Again, we are deciding to feel this way, based not so much on what is happening around us, but with what is happening within us.

I pray with my children every night, and have taught

them to express their gratitude for our home, our friends, our family, the beds we sleep in, and the food we eat.

Even my five-year-old gets in the habit of being grateful when he prays. Of course he's thankful for his school, teachers, family, and friends, but what tickles me most—what he's most grateful for—are his little race cars. He thanks God every night for those cars, as well as his other favorite toys. This is what is important in his life right now, and he's making a conscious effort to be grateful for them. He knows not all children have the privileges that he has, and he knows some might not even have race cars, or any toys at all, for that matter.

Our bodies respond with a powerful, positive sensation when we express our gratitude; it is that sensation that creates happiness.

Focusing on good things makes us feel good

Think of your brain as a magnet. What are you attracting in your life? If you put "junk" in your brain, it's going to attract more "junk." If you fill it with more of what you want in life, however, that is exactly what you are going to attract.

Have you ever noticed that people who are usually grouchy, negative, or unhappy generally seem to be involved in a variety of crises? Most of the time, their lives seem to be falling apart. It's almost as if they actually attract accidents and other unfortunate events that keep holding them back from whatever they're attempting to achieve. Part of their dialogue, if you listen closely, is that they "expect bad things to happen."

The "brain magnet" does a very good job picking up all those "bad things" and delivering them into that person's pockets!

Focus on what you don't want and you can be sure that's exactly what you'll get.

Reverse the coin. Those who are positive, upbeat and friendly tend to know what they want and get it. They also freely express their gratitude. The Grouchy Ones will say these people are "lucky," but I believe it's just our brain magnet doing its job, as instructed.

These people also know the power of positive affirmations. If we compare our minds to a computer, and if we are familiar with computer technology, we can easily understand the concept of "computer sweeps" when we clean the hard drive and get rid of all the junk that's slowing us down and blocking the free flow of data/energy.

We know the difference between saving files we appreciate and that have positive value for us, versus deleting the spam and other trash. The net result is a mind/hard drive that is rich with exciting goals and visions and dreams—all of which we truly believe we can achieve or actualize.

The gift of receiving

Has anyone ever paid you a compliment that you didn't accept? For example, has someone told you your new dress is very becoming and you responded by saying, "Oh, this old thing?"

Maybe at work someone complimented you on a job well done and you responded, "It was nothing."

Why is it often difficult to accept a compliment? Why can't we be grateful and just say "thank you"?

When we decline a compliment, we think we are being humble, but the message it delivers to our subconscious is altogether different.

Rejection of a compliment sends a message to the brain that we are *not* pretty, or smart, or hard working! This response also makes the person who paid us the compliment feel bad because we didn't accept it.

When we are grateful and accept the kind words someone has given us, it makes us feel good inside. That compliment is stored in our "hard drive," and continues to deliver positive energy.

Have an attitude of gratitude. Make a choice to be grateful and happy. Be grateful for the job you have, even if you are not happy in that job. Be grateful for your co-workers, even though they may drive you crazy. Be grateful for your boss who is hard on you, but also challenges you, and makes you stretch further than you thought you could.

I guarantee if you will start being grateful for the things in your life that make you happy, or even unhappy, you will experience a wonderful upsurge of new energy.

Suddenly, change is in the air! You might arrive at work one day and notice that you really do enjoy your job and appreciate the uniqueness of your co-workers. You might even think everyone else has changed, but it's really you who flipped the switch to the Happiness Channel.

Why not give that flip-switch a try? The alternative is staying exactly where you are; and if that doesn't feel good, you have nothing to lose and *everything* to gain.

Laughter—the greatest gift of all

When I was a kid, I loved to visit my dad's family because they always seemed so happy. Even though they were hard working people who had their share of struggles growing up, they were so upbeat and content with their lives.

My grandmother, Margaret Arnott, was a wonderful lady who had eight children. She was happily married to my grandfather, James Arnott, until the night of their 25th wedding anniversary when he suffered a heart attack and died. He was only 46; my father was only five years old at that time.

My grandmother was left without a husband or income. With a large family and no savings, she had no choice but to take her first full-time job. Her life then changed dramatically. In addition to being a single parent and homemaker, she also became a hard-working breadwinner. The brothers and sisters helped out during these troublesome times, creating a strong family bond.

It was this bond that gave them strength to make it on their own. Also, in spite of tough circumstances, these wonderful people still managed to be happy. I think I figured out why. They all have a great sense of humor; they always seem to find things to laugh about.

Most of the time they laugh over things they could cry about, such as losing a loved one; but they always seem to find a funny way to get through it. I love their energy because it's so much more fun to be around happy people than miserable ones. I also feel more comfortable with them because I think I inherited some of my dad's "corny" sense of humor.

My mom's side of the family had their share of struggles but, unlike my dad's family, they didn't have the gift of humor. My grandparents, Tom and Marie Simon, were wonderful, loving people, and they were good parents to their eight kids. Of course, my mom had the advantage over my dad of being raised by both a mother and father, but from what I'm told, they were very strict with their kids.

My mom is one of the most loving, sweet, and encouraging persons I've ever met, but she came from a stressful household which shaped much of her personality as an adult. Her parents worried and fretted over just about everything, and that stress caused tension, anxiety, and insecurity among the siblings.

My mom candidly admits that she doesn't know how to have fun. Silliness was not encouraged in her childhood home, so, unlike my father's household in which laughter was daily fare; my mom didn't have a chance to "act like a child." Fortunately, she has spent the better part of her life focusing on letting go of that stress, and learning to have fun.

My mom came from a middle class family, and didn't experience as much of the money stress of my dad's family. Why was it then, that my mom's house lacked laughter and happiness, while my dad's family joked their way through everything, including hardship?

You guessed it. Money has nothing to do with happiness. The two are totally unrelated. Some of the richest people don't know how to laugh, and the reverse is also true.

Also, my mom's family didn't have the ability to see the humor in difficult situations. Laughter and humor can lighten any situation. It may not change what is happening, but it will change the way you feel about what is happening.

There really is no right or wrong way to be raised, but having humor to get through the hard times certainly makes it easier on everyone involved. I feel that I'm fortunate to have experienced both sets of families because it helps me choose the type of environment I want to create and maintain for my own family.

Is there a secret to happiness?

No. All you have to do is decide to be happy and then make choices that will support that decision.

The song I mentioned at the beginning of the chapter has it right; we all need to stop worrying and just be happy. Maybe we could change the lyrics to: "Don't Worry, Laugh, and Be Happy!" Life would be a lot more fun if we all decided to live by those words.

Make the decision today to change how you respond to life. Laugh and enjoy each and every moment, good or bad. Make the decision to *be* happy!

Chapter Seven

Get Started Now!

I tend to procrastinate. I can start my day with the best of intentions to get important tasks done, but I soon find myself detouring from the path. I end up filling my hours with busyness and errands. I know the most important things I need to do, and the ones that will bring me ultimate happiness; but I tend to put the more pressing things first, such as chores, errands, phone calls, etcetera.

I procrastinated about writing the final chapter of this book, for example. I knew what I wanted to say, but found excuses about writing it down on paper. I seemed to be too busy with less important tasks, so it didn't get done.

People are usually aware of those times when they're procrastinating, but they can't seem to flip the switch. This can lead to all kinds of self-defeating thoughts and feelings of guilt, eventually causing depression. When we are procrastinating, it's usually over the things that will make our lives better. Not doing them usually results in unpleasant consequences.

So, why do we procrastinate? Why do we let meaningless

situations get in the way of our dreams? Why do we put off starting a new business, losing the weight, or taking that trip? What is really so important in life that we have to put our dreams on the back burner?

Who's calling the shots?

You. You are the one who procrastinates, and you are the one who can make it stop.

There are many reasons why people procrastinate, and most of them are valid excuses. Some may have a hard time concentrating, and find themselves with so much on their plate, they can't focus on just one thing. Others may have anxieties about completing a project and doing it right, so they avoid doing it all together.

Our belief about ourselves is another reason why we may procrastinate. If a person doesn't believe they can achieve their dreams, they will tell themselves so, and avoid trying.

For some, it could be the fear of failing. Why start out to accomplish something, only to realize you can't do it after all—and then, there's always the possibility that someone won't like it.

Whatever the reasons for procrastination, there are ways to overcome it.

First, take a close look at yourself and identify any behaviors that could be related to fear, anxiety, concentration or time management. Understand why you have these behaviors and try to eliminate them.

Understand your goals and your purpose. What is it you really want to accomplish? How do you want to live, act and feel?

Line up those goals with your current behavior and note where you are self-sabotaging your own dreams. Are you subconsciously creating behaviors and situations that will ultimately lead to failure?

Practice discipline and motivation

Discipline and motivation are also vital to overcoming procrastination. Ask anyone whom you consider successful how they manage to continuously work on their goals, and never stop until they reach the finish line. I bet they'll say it takes discipline to stay focused and keep going even when the going is tough or unpleasant.

Practice focusing on the reward and not on the work. Remember that the work is just a "means to an end." It's what you have to do to get what you want.

I was talking to an expectant mother a few months ago, and she asked me about the pain of labor. She was nervous about going through the experience, as this was her first delivery, and she'd heard horror stories.

I was honest with her. "Look at it this way," I told her. "The labor is just a 'means to an end.' If you don't go through the labor, then you'll never meet that precious baby!"

I encourage you to use that same advice with your own goals. Focus on the end result. Figure out what you have to do to get there, and then make those tasks a priority each day. Do the work and reap the rewards! The hard work is just the means to an end. It's what will bring you to ultimate victory.

There is no time like the present for you to become who you were born to be, and declare that you are a "Winner in Life Now!"

Dust off your dreams

Most people have dreams. Some might not put them into action but they still have them, pushed into the recesses of their minds. "Some day," they'll tell you, "I will accomplish …."

What are they waiting for? Why do they settle for living a mediocre life rather than an exceptional one? Why do they think they will do those things "later"? Why do they wait to really live to their fullest?

"Tom" was in his mid-forties. He was outwardly handsome, fit, and appeared to be leading a happy and successful life. He spent a lot of time taking care of himself by eating right, exercising, and spending time with his family. He also made personal time to relax. He worked hard to balance his life between career and family, and his kids seemed to be very happy and well-adjusted.

At Tom's annual physical, which he had skipped for the past four years, his doctors found a lump that was questionable. His doctor assured him that it was probably nothing to worry about, but just to make certain the lump was benign, he sent a sample to the lab for further analysis.

Tom and his wife spent three anxious days waiting for the results. When the doctor finally called Tom, he requested that he schedule another appointment to see him.

Perceiving it must be serious if he was being asked to make another visit to the doctor's office, Tom and his wife prepared for the worst. Unfortunately, they were right. The lump was a malignant tumor, and Tom's cancer was already in its advanced stages. The doctor told Tom he had approximately six months to live.

Tom spent several days going through the natural grief process. First, he was in disbelief and then he was overcome by unbearable sadness about leaving his family. This was followed by anger that such a tragic thing could be happening to him.

Finally, he came to the understanding that this was something he couldn't stop by complaining about it, so he decided to take action.

Tom spent the next six months loving his wife and kids more than he had during their entire time together.

He showered them with attention and time and love to let them know how much they meant to him. He prayed more than he ever had before, asking God to take care of his family when it was time for him to go.

Tom also spent time doing the things that he loved. One of those activities was writing. After the kids were asleep, Tom wrote down all the things he wanted to say to them, as their dad. He told stories about when they were babies, and he wrote about their fun trips and vacations they'd had through the years. He wrote about the future as well, and how life might be once he is gone.

He gave them advice and wisdom that he'd hoped to pass down as they grew; but since he wouldn't be with them during those times, he put it in writing for them to read when they were ready.

Tom also reconciled a strained relationship with his father. By mending this bond, Tom gave his dad the greatest gift of all: the opportunity to be with his son until the very end.

Tom died six-and-a-half months after the doctor told him the terrible news. The family was obviously devastated, but there was also a sense of peace and gratitude for the quality time they'd been able to spend with their dad and husband during those final months. They had not focused on anything other than just loving one another and doing what made them happy.

Close to the end of Tom's time, he told his wife that he was surprisingly thankful for this prognosis of only having six months to live. Without it he would have never experienced the joy of *really living.*

What are you waiting for?

What if the doctor told you that you had only six months to live? What would you do? How would you act? What would be the most important things you would want to accomplish?

No one wants to think their time is up tomorrow or the day after, but the truth is, we all have a prognosis of death. We are all going to die one day and leave our loved ones behind.

Given the same circumstances as Tom, undoubtedly we would also make the best use of our time. *But—what about now?* Why not start living that way now? Why wait another day just living an ordinary life, when you could be living an extraordinary one? What is holding you back? *What are you waiting for?*

Here's another way to think about it. What if you didn't die in six months but instead you lived to be 105? How do you want to spend all those years? Do you want to age with regret? Do you want to mourn the loss of your dreams? There will come a day when you won't have the energy mentally or physically to go after your goals, so time is of the essence.

Start living now!

Start living a life of purpose today! If you continue down the same path you are on today, tomorrow will be as predictable as today. If you live to be 105, that is a very long time to live just an ordinary life. Think about it.

About nine years ago, our family went through a devastating loss. My mother-in-law, Cindy Abernathy died in a car accident. I can't begin to describe the pain and devastation we all went through.

I was nine months pregnant with our first son and Cindy's first grandchild. He was the joy of everyone's lives and we all couldn't wait until he arrived. The night before the accident, I went to see my doctor and to my delight he said I was already well on my way. He thought I would probably deliver him that coming weekend. I can remember calling my in-laws to tell them the wonderful news. Our baby was finally coming and would be here in just a few days!

Cindy was scheduled to go on a business trip that weekend, but she was more than willing to cancel it to be with us. It was a relatively new job for my mother-in-law and I knew it was important to her, so I told her I'd call her in the morning to let her know how I felt. If my contractions started increasing, Cindy said she'd cancel the trip.

I was never able to make that call. The date was Thursday, September 9, 1999. I had great expectations about that date because I thought it would be really cool if my son was born on 9-9-99. However, that date seemed to be set for a very different event.

My parents were the ones to give me the news. My father-in-law was concerned how it would affect me and the baby, so he thought it was best if I heard the news in person rather than over the phone. At the time, my in-laws lived a few hours from us, so my father-in-law was not able to tell me right away. He called my parents and they immediately drove to my house.

There is no way to describe how I felt when I heard the news. Chris and his Mom were very close. I couldn't fathom the thought of having to tell him that his mother was gone and she'd never get to meet his first-born son. Yet this was to be my responsibility, as I had been told first about the tragedy.

The rest of that day was a blur. Family members gathered to grieve and discuss plans. In tears, I immediately called my doctor and asked for help.

I was so excited about having this baby, but now all I wanted to do was stop him from coming. I couldn't bear the thought of Chris having to welcome his new-born baby and bury his mother on the same day.

Because I was so overcome by grief, and these feelings could easily trigger labor, it was so important to keep myself as calm as possible. The doctor advised that I stay quietly lying down at all times.

This wasn't easy, but I wanted to do whatever I could for both my husband and son.

I know my prayers were answered because Austin was born 13 days after Chris's mother died. I considered it a miracle for a baby that was expected to arrive in just a day or two to have held back for 13 more days. I have no doubt this miracle came from a wonderful doctor and a lot of prayer. Thirteen days is not much time, but it was enough to separate these two dramatically life-changing events.

Live each day to the fullest

The preciousness of life becomes so apparent during those moments of departure and arrival; priorities suddenly become crystal clear. I learned how quickly life can change, and how short our time here on Earth really is. None of us has any guarantee that we have even one more day until our time is up.

So, why do we live like we have all the time in the world?

Recently I sat with a woman in her mid-eighties, now in a nursing home. She told me wonderful stories about her life as a young woman. She reminisced about times when she was free to do as she pleased. That privilege had now been taken away.

Later that night when I was recalling her words, I realized that I don't want to have regrets when I reach that woman's age. I want to tell my grandchildren the stories of everything I've accomplished. I want to be proud of the legacy I'll leave behind. I want to live each day to the fullest, right now.

Most young people want to be older. I can remember wanting to be sixteen so I could drive, or twenty-one to be considered legal. I couldn't wait to graduate from college and get my first job. Then I longed to be married, have children and "a house with a white picket fence." I kept thinking of everything I wanted in the future, rather than enjoying what was happening in the present.

Those who are older typically wish they were younger. They wish their body moved as quickly as it did before. They wish their mind could remember like it used to. If only they had the same reserves of energy now as in earlier years. *Often they wish they would have gone after their dreams when they had the opportunity.*

WHY WAIT?

Why put off your dreams until tomorrow when you can accomplish them today? Will something magical happen "later" that will give you more time, energy or desire? Probably not. So—what are you waiting for?

Life can be so busy. Even if we have some down time, we can easily fill it up with "stuff." Let's face it: life will *always* be busy. There will always be an errand to run or an obligation to fulfill.

If we know we will always be busy, then why not get started now? Why delay happiness? Why not be happy *while* you're busy? Just make the decision. **You can do this.**

The Last Lecture

Many of you may have been as inspired as I was by Professor Randy Pausch's best selling book, *The Last Lecture*. The following is quoted from the publisher's website:

> On September 18, 2007, computer science professor Randy Pausch stepped in front of an audience of 400 people at Carnegie Mellon University to deliver a last lecture called "Really Achieving Your Childhood Dreams." With slides of his CT scans beaming out to the audience, Randy told his audience about the cancer that is devouring his pancreas and that will claim his life in a matter of months. On the stage that day, Randy was youthful, energetic, handsome, often cheerfully, darkly funny. He seemed invincible. But this was a brief moment, as he himself acknowledged.
>
> Randy's lecture has become a phenomenon, as has the book he wrote, based on celebrating the dreams we all strive to make realities. Sadly, Randy lost his battle to

pancreatic cancer on July 25th, 2008, but his legacy will continue to inspire us for generations to come.

Life is short, but if we focus on the opportunities we have while we're living, then we can have a life of greatness. Rather than running from the fear of dying, make it your goal to do everything you want to do in life. Live with more purpose. Focus on your goals.

Love those you love with a love that will last them a lifetime. And most important of all: **love yourself.** Love yourself enough to follow your dreams and be who you were born to be. Live now, while you're still in "the living years."

Chapter Eight

Keep On Keeping On!

I'M not sure who originally came up with the saying, "Keep On Keeping On," but the first time I heard it was in Plano, Texas, at a lunch networking group called PowerLunch. The speaker was John West, who happened to be a friend of Zig Ziglar. I was working for Mr. Ziglar at the time, and each week a large group from the company would attend this lunch to hear some amazing speakers.

John hosted the lunch and he always ended each week by saying, "Keep On Keeping On!"

I love that saying because even though it's simple, it means so much. Life is tough, and from our limited perspective, it may not seem fair. Bad things happen to good people, and good things happen to bad people. It doesn't seem fair, but it's life.

If we dwell on everything that's wrong—if we keep finding flaws—then how can we ever start winning in life? It takes effort, determination, and persistence to focus on the good.

You're worth it and deserve the best. You deserve to

have your dreams come true. You must commit, you must believe, and you must execute your goals. *You must "Keep On Keeping On."*

When I was a child, I loved rainbows. Like most young girls, I drew them on just about anything I could find. I loved having all the bright colors reaching through the sky, with the sun glowing down on them. My drawings always had a big pot of gold at the end of the arch. I imagined those rainbows would bring me to that pot of gold.

My pot of gold is also your pot of gold. It's our happiness, our success, our joy, our prosperity. It's the compilation of all our dreams, goals, and desires *becoming real.*

In *The Wizard of Oz,* Dorothy sang about a land far above the clouds where her dreams came true, where there were no problems, and life was sweet. She knew this rainbow would lead her to wonderful places and experiences far beyond her imagination. It was within reach.

> Somewhere over the rainbow;
> Skies are blue—
> And the dreams that you dare to dream
> Really do come true!

Rainbows are beautiful and can create happiness for those who see them. But, as wonderful as these rainbows really are, do you know how they're created? By rain! Lots and lots of rain!! Sometimes even storms produce these beautiful, almost magical rainbows.

Storms can be harsh and damaging. Rain is not much better; it's wet, dismal, and often cold. It's not much fun to be out in this kind of weather, or have to suffer through a rainy, miserable day. On those days, you might want to stay at home in bed with the covers pulled over your head.

GET OUT OF BED!

I urge you, however, to get out of bed; don't miss out on that rainbow! The *only* time to see a rainbow is *after* the storm is over.

In other words, *you have to experience a lot of rain in order to see a rainbow.* Wouldn't you agree that may also be true in real life?

We all have challenges, or rainy days. Some days it's just a light, wet rain. Other times it's like a hurricane whipping up through our lives, and destroying everything it touches. The storms will come. It will rain a lot!

Even though we may prefer sunshine over rain, at some point we realize that it is the "down days" that can bring us to new places of understanding and wisdom. We can use these times to consciously practice "flipping over" our anger to understanding and forgiveness, and our sadness to joy and gratitude. This simple exercise has the power to transform those challenging situations.

Think of challenges as a "means to an end." We will struggle, we will have trouble, we will cry, we will hurt;

nothing will change that. But, if we see those trials as opportunities to bring us closer to what we want to *be, do,* and *have* in life, then it makes everything so much easier.

It is the "rain" that produces our "rainbows," and our storms that bring us to a state of appreciation for the beauty of that greater plan. This plan is designed to help us grow and learn from our mistakes. And, "believe it or not," it is this grand plan that will bring us to the land of rainbows where dreams really do come true.

Don't just wish for this golden place and don't try to convince yourself that only other people's dreams come true. Believe that your rainbow will bring you to your pot of gold. Stop running from the rain and start running to your rainbow!

Get out your umbrella because you're definitely going to need it. Get a rain coat, and maybe some galoshes. Do whatever you need to, in order to prepare for those storms, so you will move through them with courage and confidence.

Have some fun, too, on those rainy days. Jump in the puddles! Try to find the good in every challenging situation. Focus on the end result and keep your mind set on your "rainbow."

That rainbow really is there for you, and it really does want to bring you to your pot of gold. It wants you to bask in the sunshine.

You have the power to be strong. You have the power to get through the storm and delight in the rainbow.

You have the power to make it happen.

I hope you have many pots of gold in your life, and many rainbows. I also wish for you some stormy weather to help you get beyond where you are today—to help you build character and grow as an individual.

Most of all, I wish for you many raincoats and umbrellas to protect you through these storms. It's through that growth and development that you will see your rainbow. It will bring you to greater levels and allow you to seize your pot of gold. It is that pot of gold that will produce in you greatness and success beyond your expectations.

It starts with you

How will you face your storms of life? How will you prepare for all the success and happiness that is destined for you?

I believe you will conquer these storms. I believe you will run toward your rainbow!

And I really do believe you want more for yourself.

I believe you are on your way to "WINNING IN LIFE!"

It's time for *you* to believe.

Now, go make it happen!

About the Author

MICHELLE Prince launched her professional career in the sales division of the Zig Ziglar Corporation. Receiving numerous awards, including Salesperson of The Year, Michelle was able to take her passion for personal development and match it with her expertise in sales. Michelle spent the majority of her twenty-year sales career in Information Technology and Software; she has received multiple awards and accolades with a proven track record of success in sales.

The appearance of *Winning in Life Now* marks the launch of Michelle's motivational speaking and coaching enterprise. "Because I am passionate about self-development, training, and self-esteem building programs, I decided to create my own program," states Michelle. "Any techniques and strategies that can help another person become more of who God created them to be is *exciting* to me!! I'm a life-long learner, and love to discover ways to be the best me that I can be."

Michelle and her husband, Chris live in McKinney, Texas with their two wonderful boys. Her website is www.

winninginlifenow.com and she can be reached at info@princeperformance.com.

Michelle's Favorite Motivational Products

Books

Peale, Norman Vincent, *The Power of Positive Thinking*, Fireside Press, 2007.

Ziglar, Zig, *Over the Top*, Thomas Nelson, 1997.

Ziglar, Zig, *See You At The Top 25th Anniversary Edition*, Thomas Nelson (rev.), 2000.

CDs, Videos and other Products

Downey, Tina – MySuccessBox® goal setting system - www.mysuccessbox.com

Tracy, Brian – Psychology of Achievement – 6 CD set www.briantracy.com

Tracy, Brian – The Science of Self-Confidence – 6 CD set www.briantracy.com

Ziglar, Zig – How To Stay Motivated (Volumes I, II & III) with Performance Planner www.ziglar.com

Notes

NOTES

Notes

Notes

NOTES